Here a baa, there a cluck, everywhere a quack-quack

**THE ORIGINAL INDESTRUCTIBLES®**

For ages 0 and

## BOOKS BABIES CAN REALLY SINK THEIR GUMS INTO!

Listen to the pigs: *Oink, oink!*
The cows are next: *Moo, moo!*
Now everyone chime in: *Ee-I-Ee-I-Oh!*

Sing along with the whole farm in a book that's INDESTRUCTIBLE.

*Dear Parents*: INDESTRUCTIBLES are built for the way babies "read": with their hands and mouths. INDESTRUCTIBLES won't rip or tear and are 100% washable. They're made for baby to hold, grab, chew, pull, and bend.

CHEW ALL THESE AND MO

$5.99 US / $8.99 Can.
ISBN 978-1-5235-1773-2
9 781523 517732   505

Copyright © 2022 by Indestructibles, LLC. Used under license.
Illustrations copyright © 2022 by Workman Publishing Co., Inc.
All rights reserved.
Library of Congress Cataloging-in-Publication Data is available.
WORKMAN is a registered trademark of Workman Publishing Co., Inc.
First printing November 2022 | 10 9 8 7 6 5 4 3 2 1

All INDESTRUCTIBLES books have been safety-tested and m
exceed ASTM-F963 and CPSIA guid
INDESTRUCTIBLES is a registered trademark of Indestructibles
Contact specialmarkets@workman.com rega
special discounts for bulk purch
Printed in

**WORKMAN PUBLISHING CO., INC.** 225 Varick Street, New York, NY 10014 • indestructiblesinc.com